# Odysseus and the Magic of Circe

## Tales from the Odyssey

*Written by I. M. Richardson*
*Illustrated by Hal Frenck*

**Troll Associates**

*Library of Congress Cataloging in Publication Data*

Richardson, I. M.
   Odysseus and the magic of Circe.

   (Tales from the Odyssey / adapted by I. M. Richardson; bk. 4)
   Summary: Odysseus's listeners hear him describe his
visit with the goddess Circe and his journey to the
underworld.
   [1. Mythology, Greek]  I. Frenck, Hal, ill.
II. Homer.  Odyssey.  III. Title.  IV. Series: Richardson, I. M. Tales from the Odyssey; bk. 4.
PZ8.1.R396Tal  1984  bk. 4  292'.13s  [292'.13]  83-14237
ISBN 0-8167-0011-7 (lib. bdg.)
ISBN 0-8167-0012-5 (pbk.)

"Fill your cup again," said the queen. "And continue your tale," added the king. Their guest lifted his cup and took a sip. His throat was dry from telling of his adventures. His eyes were moist from remembering his lost companions.

3

His name was Odysseus, King of the Greek island of Ithaca, hero of the Trojan War. Although nearly ten years had passed since the war had ended, he had not yet returned home. Poseidon, the angry god of the sea, had delayed Odysseus by creating one misfortune after another for the poor traveler.

Odysseus had just finished telling his host and hostess how
he had lost eleven of his twelve ships in the Land of the
Giants. "From there," he explained, "we continued on our
homeward course. But Poseidon's anger had not yet died.
He had more troubles in store for us.

"We soon came upon a lovely island in the middle of the sea. I guided our ship into a broad harbor and dropped anchor. We went up onto the beach and stayed there, resting for two days and two nights. On the morning of the third day, I set off to explore the island.

"About midday, I reached the top of a lofty peak, from which I could see the entire island. Smoke was rising from a wooded glen in the distance. Who lived there? What was this place called? Many questions came into my mind. I decided to return to the ship and send some men into the glen to seek the answers.

"When I told them what I had seen, there was no end to their moaning and wailing. They remembered what had happened the last time we had visited an unknown land. At that time, I had sent three men to find out who the inhabitants were. As a result, all our companions had been eaten by giants. Would the same thing happen to us again?

"This time, I divided my men into two groups. I picked a
sailor to command one group, and I headed the other one
myself. We drew lots to see who would stay with the ship,
and who would go inland. Soon the sailor was leading his
men away, moaning and weeping at their uncertain fate.

"When they came to the glen, they saw a mysterious stone dwelling. From inside this strange place came a lovely song —but it was the voice of a terrible goddess named Circe. In the clearing outside were wolves, tigers, lions, and other beasts. My men were terrified, as you can well imagine.

"But the beasts were as tame as puppies. They came up to my men, wagging their tails. They had once been human beings themselves, but Circe had used her magic to turn them into beasts. Suddenly, the beautiful goddess herself came to the door. 'Come in,' she said. 'Let me offer you food and drink.'

"They all went inside, except for their leader. He suspected a trick of some kind, and hid outside. The rest sat down at a long table that was set with cheeses and good things to eat. Circe brought them warm drinks that she had sweetened with honey. But she had also put something else in— something magical.

"Soon they had drained their cups. Circe went from one to the other, tapping each man with her magic wand. At once, they began turning into pigs. Before long, the room was filled with grunts, bristles, and curly tails. Then she shooed them into pens, and tossed them some acorns and other things that pigs are fond of.

"When the sailor who was their leader saw what had become of his men, he returned to the ship. Tears of grief rolled down his cheeks as he told us of the fate of his men. Then I took my bow and my bronze sword, and I started off toward the wooded glen.

"As I approached Circe's house, who should I meet but Hermes, the messenger of the gods. He gave me a magical flower and said, 'This will protect you from Circe's magic. Wait until she taps you with her wand, and then draw your sword. Tell her that you will kill her unless she promises not to work her magic on you.'

"As soon as Hermes had returned to Mount Olympus, I went to Circe's house and called out to her. The goddess opened the door and greeted me, just as she had done earlier with my men. I followed her inside and sat down. She brought me a magical drink and smiled wickedly as I drank it.

"Then she tapped me with her wand and said, 'Now join your friends in the pigpens!' But instead of grunting and sprouting bristles, I jumped up and drew my sword. Circe cried out, 'Ah! You must be Odysseus, King of Ithaca. Hermes told me you would stop here on your way home from Troy. Come, let us be friends.'

"'Before I put down my sword,' I said, 'you must promise that you will not try to trick me or harm me in any way.' She agreed at once to this demand, so I laid down my weapon. Then the goddess ordered her maids to prepare a warm, soothing bath for me.

"When I was refreshed, Circe led me to a table where a feast was laid out. Although the food looked delicious, I did not touch it. 'What is wrong, Odysseus?' asked the goddess. And I replied, 'I cannot think of eating as long as my men are held under your magical spell. You must free them.'

"'That is easily done,' said the goddess. She opened the pen and let the grunting, squealing pigs out into the room. Then she rubbed a magical ointment on them, and they immediately lost their bristles and curly tails. Soon they were men again.

"They were so glad to see me that they grasped my hands and began to dance around the room. Circe was so touched by their behavior that she said, 'Odysseus, go down to the harbor and pull your ship up onto the beach. Stow your goods in a cave and bring the rest of your men back here.'

"I returned at once to my ship. The men I had left there had given me up for lost, so when they saw me they were overjoyed. They were eager to find out about their missing companions and asked one question after another. 'I will take you to them,' I said. 'But first, we must beach our ship and hide our belongings in a cave.'

"We set to work at once, but the sailor who had seen Circe did everything he could to stop us. He was convinced that Circe had me in her power, and that this was just one of her tricks. 'Stop!' he cried. 'Can't you see what is happening? You will all be turned into pigs or lions or wolves!'

"But in the end, he returned to Circe's home with us. When he saw his companions feasting happily, he knew that it was not a trick. Then we all helped ourselves to the good food and drink. We had soon forgotten the many misfortunes we had suffered.

"Circe made our stay so comfortable that we remained with her for an entire year. But at last it was time for us to go. 'First, you must make another journey,' said the goddess as we prepared to leave. 'You must visit the Kingdom of the Dead. There, you must seek advice from the ghost of the blind prophet of Thebes.'

"We left at once. The North Wind blew our ship to the edge of the world. From there, we continued on foot to the Underworld. Soon we reached the place where the River of Fire and the River of Grief rush into the River of Pain. I dug a pit and made a sacrifice to the gods. Then the ghosts of the dead approached.

"Finally, the ghost of the blind prophet appeared. He came up to me and said, 'Poseidon is still angry because you have blinded his son. If you want to reach home safely, make sure you do not harm the cattle of the sun god when you stop at his island. If you harm them in any way, your ship and crew will be destroyed.'

"Then the prophet added, 'If these things come to pass, you will arrive home later—aboard another man's ship. You will find great troubles in your house, and you will kill the troublemakers. After that, you shall find peace at last.'

"When the ghosts of the dead had gone, I returned to my ship, and my men leaned into their oars. They rowed until we found a breeze that filled the sails and carried us back to Circe's island. That night, we slept on the beach. It felt good to be back in the world of the living again.

"At dawn, Circe came and joined us, bringing plenty of food and drink. I told her all about our visit to the Underworld, and when I had finished, she took me aside. 'Listen to me, Odysseus,' she said. 'Tomorrow you will be leaving here. But first, I will tell you what dangers lie before you, and how you may avoid further misfortune.'

"She told me of the Sirens, whose sweet songs lure men to their death. She spoke of the Moving Rocks, and how they could smash to splinters any ship that came near. She told of the six-headed monster named Scylla, who ate passing sailors. And she warned me of Charybdis, the whirlpool that swallowed ships down to the bottom of the sea.

"The next day, we left Circe's island," continued Odysseus. "We put our ship on a homeward course. This time, however, I knew of the dangers that lay ahead and how to avoid them. This time, I knew that we would soon arrive safely on the shores of our beloved homeland."